THE VILLAGES OF
Suffolk

MARK MITCHELS

COUNTRYSIDE BOOKS

Other counties in this series include:

HAMPSHIRE
HERTFORDSHIRE
SURREY

For Peter, Sarah and Edward

First published 1999
© Mark Mitchels 1999

COUNTRYSIDE BOOKS
3 CATHERINE ROAD
NEWBURY, BERKSHIRE

ISBN 1 85306 598 6

Designed by Mon Mohan
Produced through MRM Associates Ltd., Reading
Printed in Singapore

Contents

INTRODUCTION

It may be convenient to speak of the typical Suffolk village but, of course, there is no such place. However hard we try to produce an Identikit settlement we are doomed to fail, and rightly so. The diversity of the village is its greatest strength. Some may indeed possess timber framed, pink-washed, thatched roofed medieval treasures, snuggling below the lofty flint tower of a Perpendicular church, but that does not make them better villages, or more successful ones. Buildings are part of the story, but without people even the prettiest cluster of houses becomes pointless. Villages are communities, which live and breathe. A line of dull red brick houses beside a main road can be home to energetic, friendly and compassionate families who put their more photogenic neighbours to shame. Of course it's impossible to generalise, but that is the point – as we drive through the villages of Suffolk we must not expect to discover everything about them at a glance.

Producing a book of photographs of Suffolk villages is asking for trouble anyway. There are those which have to be included, because to leave them out would inflict a sort of county shame. Then there are the ones which are not so well known, but still attractive enough to warrant inclusion and wider appreciation. Finally there are the majority which may not please the lens, but are equally worthwhile in every other respect.

Once the village was centred on the church, school and pub. Now in many cases only the last survives, and that has experienced the wind of change. People no longer go to church or chapel in the numbers they once did, and the schools are larger and centred on local towns. Even the pub can no longer rely on the regulars to pay the bills, but advertises in local newspapers to attract diners from far afield, and promotes its food, children's play area and car boot sale beside its Good Ale Guide entry. But the wonder is that the village endures – it meets each new threat and somehow manages to keep going.

This book is a celebration of the Suffolk village. Here are no film sets, designed to be seen from one angle only, and closed to the public when the weather is bad. People live in them, and are fiercely loyal to what they know and love. They are proud of the lovely old buildings, and take a justifiable pleasure when visitors congratulate them on the view, but they see beyond the postcards. The village hall is seldom on the tourist route, but throughout the year it acts as the centre of the community. It need not be pretty or even old, but it witnesses the good times and the bad. It is a place for sharing, and that is what the village has always been good at. In the end, the scenery may have stood still, but the Suffolk villager is too sensible to do the same.

Wortham and Palgrave

*'Certainly a Suffolk hedgerow full of honeysuckle and dog roses is hard to beat in
Nature.'* Hugh Farmer, *The Cottage in the Forest.*

Wortham is a village on a grand scale: this is the largest unenclosed green in Suffolk and seems to stretch for miles. The houses occupy remote plots, and most of them are hidden behind trees and bushes. Horses tethered to enormous lengths of rope can appear to be the only residents, and they no doubt like it that way. They are very friendly.

Wortham is known in literary circles as the parish once served by the author Richard Cobbold. He was incumbent here from 1827 to 1877, which is a considerable slice of anyone's life, and he saw most of his flock arrive and depart. His verses written for the headstones in the churchyard suggest he did well to concentrate on novels.

Even in Suffolk, which was staunchly Parliamentarian during the Civil War, there are lots of King's Head pubs, so it is refreshing to learn that in Wortham there was a Dick Inn, named to commemorate Tumbledown Dick or more correctly Richard Cromwell, son of the Protector.

Just outside the village school is a magnificent brick and stone gateway, which was once an imposing entrance to the seat of learning. Today, the busy main road would cut short any child foolish enough to use it, so the weeds have taken over.

Palgrave is another village forced to come to terms with the impatience of modern traffic. It is most appropriate that in St Peter's churchyard there is the grave of John Catchpole, who died in 1787. He is depicted on his headstone driving a coach and six powerful horses.

Many of the cottages in Palgrave are beautifully preserved and restored (*inset*). Just by the charming village sign there are several which reflect the pride of their current owners.

Hoxne and Wingfield

'And now it strikes me that conversation was not much cultivated in the villages of
East Anglia in 1837, and yet there were splendid exceptions – …'
James Ewing Ritchie, *Christopher Crayon's Recollections.*

Like so many other bits of history from long ago, it rather depends on who tells you the story. The residents of Hoxne will tell you that King Edmund was killed here in AD 870. He was on the run from the Danes and hid under a bridge, only to be betrayed by his spurs glinting in the sunlight. He was tied to a tree, and killed by arrows. The church of St Peter and St Paul can produce a painted screen said to be the very tree poor Edmund was placed against!

When Farmer Peter Whatling lost a hammer while out ploughing in 1992 he asked Eric Lawes, a local gardener and metal detector user, to search for it. He found the hammer, but also uncovered a vast horde of gold and silver coins which dated from the last years of the Roman occupation. It is an amusing touch that in the British Museum the visitor can not only gaze on the sheer beauty and richness of the articles recovered, but also take a look at a very large, rather rusty hammer!

History is never far from Wingfield (*inset*), as it has that air of stepping back into the past. Horses graze on the common as they have always done, the church provides a whole exciting chapter of court intrigue, and the castle stands safe behind the waters of the moat.

The Wingfield family began as merchants of Hull in the 14th century but by ability and influence they rose to become Earls and Dukes of Suffolk. Shakespeare chronicles their performance on his stage, showing one of them at Agincourt, and another having an affair with the Queen which led to his violent death on the beach at Dover. Many of the family lie sculptured in alabaster in St Andrew's church.

Fressingfield and Laxfield

'The late 20th century with its pedestrianised precincts and its hypermarkets may be circling like the sea, awaiting its hour, but it has not yet broken through.'
Byron Rogers.

The village sign of Fressingfield shows a pilgrim and his donkey, which is a reminder that for centuries this village was on the route to Bury St Edmunds.

The Fox and Goose is a lovely rambling timber and brickwork building which stands to the side of the churchyard. The most delicious smells emanate through the windows and it has an enviable reputation for excellent food. Once it was the Guildhall of Fressingfield, but the times change and so the building was forced to adapt.

The church of St Peter and St Paul offers further evidence of the centuries merging together, for carved on the back of a pew is the name of Alice de la Pole. Her family were important in this area, and the fine porch was built by Catherine de la Pole in 1420, probably to honour her husband who died of disease during the siege of Harfleur, and her son who died at Agincourt just two months later.

Laxfield has a wonderful church and so it comes as a bit of a shock to discover that this village was the birthplace of the Puritan William Dowsing, who devoted his life to smashing up the interiors of East Anglia's churches. What makes it worse is that he was proud of his efforts and kept a detailed diary of every piece of destruction he completed.

Today, the village retains the ingredients of its past (*inset*) in a delightful cluster – All Saints' church, the Royal Oak Inn and the timber former Guildhall, now the museum. Horses and tractors can still share the main street, which confirms the impression of continuity which is so reassuring in these fast-moving times.

Thornham and Mellis

'The wheels of life are better oiled in the pleasant surroundings of Suffolk where the native is of a naturally courteous turn of mind.'
A. Swinburn, *Memories of a School Inspector.*

Everybody gets very protective of pubs, and the life and well-being of a village is almost measured in relation to the reputation that amenity enjoys. The Four Horseshoes in Thornham Magna is a lovely pub, and has a very loyal following. The importance of its role has been recognised over several centuries for on a beam is the inscription: 'When you have lost your inns drown your empty selves for you have seen the last of England.' Now that is putting the case very strongly! On the subject of pubs and trivial information about them, the bar of the

White Horse Inn in Thornham Magna is said to be only half in that village, with the rest in Stoke Ash!

The village is the seat of Lord Henniker, and one of the ancestors clearly shared Thomas Killigrew's sentiments about the pleasures of life. He went into exile with Charles II and was considered so debauched he was expelled from Venice. His reputation today is better, as he founded the Drury Lane theatre.

Thornham Parva has a thatched church, which is now quite rare. The great treasure on show here is the Retable, an altarpiece showing the crucifixion, dating from 1300. It also shows eight saints set on a gold background. One of them is East Anglia's St Edmund, holding an arrow. It is a major work of art, and so it is quite remarkable to realise how nearly it was lost. Only in 1927 during a house clearing was the masterpiece rediscovered, on its way to an auction room. It still has the sale room tag to this day.

Mellis possesses one of the great Suffolk Greens – it covers 1,400 acres, and stretches two miles. A railway line crosses it at one point, but otherwise it is open, and continues to offer grazing when required. Some very pretty cottages (*inset*) stand at the edge, often all but hidden among the tall trees, and they each bring an individual point of interest to the green.

Mendlesham and Stonham Parva

'Not only are the people shy, but the spirit of the country itself is independent, capricious and elusive …' Julian Tennyson, *Suffolk Scene*.

For many people the village of Mendlesham means just one thing – a truly enormous television mast which rises from the fields and at times really does pierce the clouds. At night it is even more distinctive when a line of red lights climbs apparently unsupported to the stars themselves. For these people the village close to the transmitter mast has a very pleasant surprise in store, for Mendlesham is full of lovely old buildings and has a street plan which makes walking a pleasure.

The main street contains several splendid timber buildings, and some of them continue to be local stores, serving the community as they were intended. As is so often the case in Suffolk, many of the houses are clearly concealing even more timber beneath their modern frontages. There is a grand village sign, which displays one of the village's other claims to fame – the Mendlesham chair. This is a particularly graceful and intricate wooden armchair, which combines the traditional elements of design with a slender appeal.

Close to the sign is the old preaching stone, which was for the benefit of travelling preachers who had to address their congregations outside because the established church refused to grant them a licence. East Anglia gave its support to Cromwell and the Puritan Revolution during the English Civil War so it is not fanciful to imagine the people of Mendlesham gathered at this place, listening attentively to a fiery sermon. In the church of St Mary there is a very fine and famous collection of armour which covers the period 1470 to 1630. It is displayed in a room over the porch. The village records speak of a muster of the local volunteers on Mellis Green in 1627, presumably carrying many of these weapons.

The Stonham Magpie is another local landmark, and must be one of the largest pub signs in the country (*inset*). Certainly there cannot be many which straddle a trunk road!

Walsham le Willows

*'If you want to comprehend village Suffolk, travel its myriad lanes and tracks, that
complex network trodden into the map by the farmers and their stock, by foresters and
children, and parsons and lovers, and craftsmen and hunters.'*
Ronald Blythe, *Our Villages* from *Suffolk for Ever.*

Any place which includes the word Willows in its name conjures up a scene of pretty houses with gardens running down to a tree-lined stream, and a mass of flower beds and greenery: in brief, a perfect English village. Walsham le Willows is all these things and more. The River Little Ouse does run through the back gardens of some of the prettiest houses in the county, and wherever you look there are ancient trees and bursts of colour from a score of cleverly laid out flower beds. So proud is this village of its skill at gardening that once a year many of its finest are opened to the public in the cause of charity, and the air resounds to both praise and envy!

At the centre stands the 15th century church of St Mary, a symbol of permanence and certainty. Inside is a most unusual survivor from an earlier age: a Virgin's Crant. This is a wooden disc suspended from the ceiling to the memory of Mary Boyce who died in November 1685, apparently after receiving a fatal wound from Cupid's arrow. The crant was a medallion which marked the pew where once sat a virgin who had died in a state of purity.

The 16th century Six Bells Inn stands opposite the church and together they care for the bodies and souls of the inhabitants. Further down the street are a number of more modern timber buildings, which curiously have stern biblical texts carved into their main beams, perhaps another determined effort to protect the well-being of the residents.

Haughley and Stowupland

'… I like Suffolk. The people are hearty, and radicalism is not quite so rampant as it is elsewhere.' Anthony Trollope, *The Way We Live Now.*

Modern Suffolk affords too many examples of villages which have suffered from being on the course of main roads, with all the attendant horrors of heavy traffic and extensive building. It is good to reflect that occasionally there are survivors, and Haughley is fortunate in being one of them. Today it stands defiant almost within earshot of the mighty A14 but nevertheless safely apart from it.

The Green is extensive and adorned with tubs of flowers which proclaim the sense of pride which is evident in Haughley. Long ago, however, this was no pleasing backwater, but a military centre of paramount importance, for soon after the Norman Conquest a motte and bailey castle was constructed to the north of the village, of which traces still remain. It stood 80 feet high and occupied a site of seven acres. Today only the moat remains, and with it the excitement of imagining that moment when the Earl of Leicester's mercenaries stormed it in 1173. It seems hard to believe on a summer day now!

In the church of St Mary there is a collection of 18th century fire buckets, which suggest an enthusiasm on the part of local people to preserve the past.

In the nearby village of Stowupland is a remarkable garden with a vast collection of water pumps, all brightly painted and displayed with fairground exuberance (*inset*).

Lovers of the novels of Thomas Hardy will appreciate this story, taken from the *Ipswich Journal* of 1787: 'A farmer of the parish of Stowupland sold his wife to a neighbour for five guineas, and being happy to think he had made a good bargain, presented her with a guinea to buy her a new gown; he then went to Stowmarket, and gave orders for the bells to be rung upon the occasion.'

Rattlesden

'There was such an infinite number [of swallows] that they covered the whole roof of the church, and of several houses near.' Daniel Defoe, *Tour of Britain.*

One of the elements which makes for a memorable village scene is the combination of buildings and greenery. Rattlesden offers to the visitor a variety of attractive views, from all directions, and most of them are centred on the lovely church of St Nicholas.

At the entrance to the churchyard there is a superb timber house, its dark oak beams contrasting sharply with its whitewashed plasterwork, and grand enough to be a guildhall or at least the residence of a local worthy. And

there are many more gathered around the church, each a reminder of the village's past importance (*inset*).

The River Ratt was navigable once, and this served as the port for Bury St Edmunds. It is supposed that the stone for the great abbey building was landed here, and then conveyed to the site by road.

By the road bridge in the village there are some enormous whalebones, which seem to require explanation, but the best available account is satisfied to note that they exist and are probably a local curiosity brought to Rattlesden in the 19th century. Better documented is the spectacular find made in 1972 when a local man was hoeing sugar beet. He scraped up a gilt bronze statuette of St John the Evangelist, which dated from 1180 and fetched £40,000 at auction.

Of less certain worth was the discovery in the 1890s of a coffin and skeleton, thought to be the remains of Robert Bumpstead who died in 1780. The mystery of his being found outside the churchyard was solved when it was noted that he had died in debt, and his body had been buried in haste to prevent its seizure by his creditors! Quite what value his mortal remains had for those to whom he owed money is not clear and the poor man's disposal is now the stuff of local legend.

Moulton and Dalham

*'Thence I passed by some woods and little villages of a few scattered houses, and
generally the people here … know scarce three miles from their home …'*
Celia Fiennes, *The Journeys of Celia Fiennes*.

Once upon a time the quiet village of Moulton with its famous Pack Horse Bridge was on a trunk road of East Anglia, for it straddled the highway from Cambridge to Bury St Edmunds. In the Middle Ages the roads were often quite impassable by wheeled vehicles for much of the year so merchants and farmers had to rely on the pack animals, which could keep moving however muddy and uneven the tracks might be.

Moulton's bridge dates from the 15th century and is very rare, probably owing its survival to the River Kennet which proved too much for later road builders and was easier to overcome elsewhere. The bridge is indeed very narrow, because animals could be taken over in single file, but the visitor who stands in the centre cannot fail to notice that it could cope with a cart width so perhaps it had a more ambitious purpose before the traffic abandoned it. There is a ford at the side, anyway, so the choice remains!

Nearby is Penny Grave where gypsies and travellers are said to place pennies on the grave of a shepherd boy who was buried at the crossroads in unconsecrated ground. He had been accused of stealing sheep and the shame drove him to suicide, and the inevitable fate of non Christian burial.

Dalham is also strung out along the River Kennet and is exquisitely pretty (*inset*). One cottage after another lines the river bank, and the profusion of thatch and timber frame is seemingly endless. At the centre stands a pub with a bridge over the water for access.

St Mary's church dates from the 14th century and when the spire fell down in the 17th century the villagers attributed the disaster to Oliver Cromwell, suggesting it happened at the very moment of his death! They paid £400 to replace it with a fine tower.

Hargrave and Ickworth

'… the triumphant crow of pheasants, the urgent call of rooks, the gentle plaint of wood pigeons, the staccato jukking of partridges … the whole air throbs with the beauty and amazement of it.'
Julian Tennyson, *Suffolk Scene.*

There can be few, if any, scenes in Suffolk which have really remained unaltered over the centuries, but these fields continue to be worked for the traditional purposes, even if the methods have changed, not least in scale.

The village of Hargrave stands for many aspects of life which have changed. Many centuries ago pilgrims passed through on their way to the great abbey at Bury St Edmunds, and then there were pack horses in their hundreds carrying goods to market, and whose drovers stopped at the Cock's Head Inn for a much-needed drink. The name is a reminder that Hargrave was known for its cock fighting. Only a century ago these fields were worked by the Suffolk Punch, and the men of Hargrave were particularly expert at coaxing the best out of them.

Ickworth Hall is the centre of a vast estate, once owned by the Earls of Bristol, but now in the care of the National Trust. To circumnavigate the property is an eleven mile journey! The entrance is in the village of Horringer (*inset*), and beside the gates stands the church of St Leonard. The village green is surrounded by pretty white cottages, many of them thatched, and there is a profusion of trees.

Church going in the early 19th century was evidently a serious business, as this account of Horringer bears witness: 'In the gangway during service time a man would stand with a wand of office. He was one of the two beadles … The other was in the gallery where the choir sang. At service time these two changed places. Their business was to restrain the young and to keep the somnolent awake.'

Rede

'Forty years ago, too, when a farmer came to buy a new farm, one of the things that he looked for on his first visit of inspection was the depth of the muck, in the yards.'
Simon Dewes, *A Suffolk Childhood.*

Upper Dods Farm (*opposite*) is typical of scores of farm houses across the county. It is built of local timber, and thatched in the traditional manner. Some may have moats, a memory of less peaceful times, but they all represent a link with agriculture that extends from the medieval period right down to our present time. Once the horse defined the work rate of the land, but now

machinery has swept them aside, joined by hedgerows and small woods. Farming has become a business, with little room for nostalgia. People who live close to the land tend not to be opposed to such changes, for their lives were always hard and unforgiving.

Suffolk is not quite so flat as unkind outsiders care to allege, but it is mostly unspectacular in the contour aspect, so to be told that Rede is the highest part of the county – at 420 feet – is worthy of passing mention. The writer M.R. James unkindly described this fact as Suffolk's greatest achievement!

With our tidy minds we expect things to be self-explanatory, cut and dried and uncomplicated. Unfortunately, that can never be the case with churches. However much we love to label them Norman, Perpendicular, Victorian or anything, every church defies such neat listing because it is the product of centuries of use, and has been altered and 'improved' to suit the times. All Saints' church at Rede (*inset*) may have Norman walls, but it also has a tower from 1300, and the chancel was built in 1874. Villages evolve and resist attempts to hold change at bay. That is what makes them special.

The Thurlows and Stradishall

*'Labourers had worked these fields for perhaps 1,000 years. They seem to slip back
into the earth ...that they had scratched for years, leaving nothing behind.'*
Ronald Blythe, *Akenfield.*

Long before Parliament took over control of schools, hospitals and welfare, it was left to local worthies to provide for the needs of their towns and villages. All over England men of wealth and importance established charities which long after their deaths continued to care for the people they had chosen. In Little Thurlow there is just such a reminder of this old system.

Sir Stephen Soame was a Thurlow man, and in course of time he went to London, prospered and rose to become Lord Mayor. But he did not forget or neglect his birthplace. By his will he left funds to endow an almshouse for nine poor people on the edge of the village, and he also founded a school which offered clever boys the opportunity to go to university and perhaps even emulate his own example! It is no longer a school, but the building stands with his crest over the door, and includes the date of its foundation – 1614. Sir Stephen was buried in St Peter's church.

Great and Little Thurlow are pretty villages which merge without a break between them and a particularly attractive spot is by the river where a cast iron bridge carries the road up towards a group of cottages.

Tucked away in the folds of the countryside are scores of wonderful cottages like this one (*inset*), at Stradishall. Many East Anglian villages were taken over by the RAF or USAF during the war, but most saw the land return to fields in due course. Here, the camp became a prison and now miles of perimeter fence confront the visitor.

In 1920 a young journalist from Chelsea, dissatisfied with city life, made a bold decision and arrived at the 500 acre farm of Mr Colville at Farley Hall near Stradishall, to learn the art of farming. Within a year Adrian Bell had purchased his own 35 acre farm nearby and began his career as a Suffolk farmer. The books he wrote about his experiences on the land have become classics, and no rural anthology is complete without them!

Stoke by Clare and Clare

'While thus we join in cheerful sound, let love and loyalty abound. Mears, London, fecit, 1779, inscribed on a bell in Clare Church.

During the 18th century the occupant of Stoke College was Sir Hervey Elwes, who was described as 'the most perfect picture of human misery that ever existed'. He inherited the property in time to discover the full extent of its debts, and he seems to have determined to return it to solvency by the simple expedient of spending nothing. When he died he was succeeded by his nephew, John, who became another eccentric miser. The property duly returned to health! His picture adorns the village sign.

There had been a Benedictine priory in the village until the Reformation, and the Elwes house incorporated parts

of the building. It is now a private school. The church of St Augustine is said to have the most beautiful pulpit in England, but it is also so small that a fat person would have difficulty turning round in it.

Clare is a beautiful village with ever-present memories of its heyday as one of the great wool towns of East Anglia. The houses embrace the fine church of St Peter and St Paul and the scale is refreshingly intimate and welcoming. The Bell Hotel was famous for making candles which were sold throughout the region. It is one of the five pubs in Clare, where once there had been thirteen. The Museum is in the Priest's House (*inset*) which dates from 1473, although the magnificent pargeting, or ornamental plaster-work, dates from the 17th century.

Clare Castle was the seat of the Earls of Clare (or Clarence) and it is suggested that they took their title from the 'clear' waters of the nearby River Stour. Now it is a ruined shell keep and forms the attractive centre of a Country Park which incorporates the former railway buildings in its grounds. During the excavations for the railway a piece of jewellery was found which had once belonged to Lionel, Duke of Clarence, second son of Edward III. Incredibly he is known to have given it to his daughter Philippa, who resided in Clare Castle.

Long Melford and Cavendish

'The general scene formed by the patches of green and the various groups of trees and houses is quite delightful, all of them, down to the smallest hovel, being trim and carefully kept.' François de la Rochefoucauld, *A Frenchman's Year in Suffolk* (trans. Norman Scarfe).

The Church of Holy Trinity is often praised as the best in Suffolk, and few would dispute that it would be one of the finalists! However, even with its Perpendicular windows – all 100 of them – it is not quite as perfect as the first glance supposes. The original tower fell down in 1710 following a storm, and was rebuilt rather badly in 1725, and had to wait until the present century before it was clad in stone.

To the right stand the Almshouses of the Holy and Undivided Trinity, which were established by William Cordell in 1573 for twelve poor men. He rose to become Speaker of the Commons during Mary's reign.

Another benefactor of the church was John Clopton of Kentwell Hall. He also has his emblem included high on the church walls, and like Cordell he was buried there. Today, during the summer, his house is the location for a quite wonderful recreation of Tudor life.

Never was the word 'Long' put to better use, for by one calculation the main street of Long Melford is over two and a half miles in length. From the old bridge to the church is over a mile, and it is worth the walking for it comprises a journey past many pretty buildings, including the medieval Bull Hotel.

Cavendish is famous for Old Hyde Park Corner – the pink-washed cottages (*inset*) which stand before the church of St Mary. They have not always looked so

appealing for in the 1950s they were in a sadly dilapidated state and eventually burnt down. What we enjoy today is a sensitive reconstruction.

The village sign displays an event from the Peasants' Revolt in 1381 when Wat Tyler, the rebel leader was killed by John Cavendish, whose father was Lord Chancellor of England and considered by some to be the architect of England's misery. This gentleman was pursued into his native Suffolk, and prudently hid all his valuables in the church tower before fleeing to the wilds of Mildenhall. It did him no good for he was taken and killed. Forty pounds of his money provided the chancel.

Lavenham

'Weaving has left us many things. Above all it has left us Lavenham, by far the most beautiful small town I have ever seen.' Julian Tennyson, *Suffolk Scene*, 1939.

Wool has been described as East Anglia's Golden Fleece, and Lavenham provides evidence of how much money there was for the few who were successful. In every street there are scores of timber frame buildings, seemingly unchanged since the date of their construction. But they are proof of Lavenham's prosperity for in the 15th century only the very rich could afford to use oak as their main building material.

This was a centre of industry in its day, and the fortunes were not made by shepherds but by the clothiers and merchants who together ensured their products reached the customers. Half a million square foot of cloth was produced here every year.

The church of St Peter and St Paul overlooks Lavenham and perfectly illustrates the complex politics that existed at the time of its building, for it represents both aristocracy and merchant, the old and the new. The tower, which is 141 feet high, was the gift of the 13th Earl of Oxford, a powerful and influential magnate.

There is no formal street plan. One of the most enduring aspects of Lavenham is its unpredictability, and the names recall the past: Lady Street (where the Spring family lived) had the magnificent Wool Hall, formerly the Guild of our Lady (*inset*). Water Street leads to the river, passing a house with a carving of a wool merchant beside the doorway. The Priory was once the home of Benedictine monks. In Old Shilling Street once lived Isaac

Taylor whose daughter wrote popular verse including *Twinkle Twinkle Little Star*!

John Constable attended the Grammar School in Lavenham but left after only a brief stay as the Master was helplessly in love and so could find no time to teach his pupils!

Anywhere and everywhere in Lavenham is a feast for the eyes, and it is entirely appropriate that the Suffolk Preservation Society should have their headquarters here, for once obtained, the golden fleece must never be lost again.

Monks Eleigh

' "We were here before the Conquest, and here we are now," might still be said by certain dwellers in Suffolk.' William White, 1865.

The past is not easily ignored in East Anglia. So it is with Monks Eleigh. There never were monks living in this village. The name recalls the time when Earldorman Brithnoth gave this part of his estates to the Dean and Chapter of Canterbury – in AD 991!

For most visitors Monks Eleigh is the quintessential English village – a cluster of pretty houses around a green, all watched over by a grand old church. There was a time when railway posters used this view of the village to attract holiday makers to the Eastern counties.

Overlooking the village is the church of St Peter which dates from the late Middle Ages. It was given a spire in 1631 – presumably because it was considered incomplete without one! In 1845 the spire was dismantled when it was considered unsafe.

The green was an important part of the village, for it was no one person's property, and so could be used for markets, fairs and all sorts of gatherings. It was in every sense the community's centre, and probably as such it rarely looked as well tended and as green as we expect today. The pump (*opposite*) was placed here in 1845 for the benefit of the villagers following the sale of some property connected with a bequest.

The darker side of village life in the past is witnessed by this entry in the parish register: 'Dec 19th 1748: Alice, the wife of Thomas Green, labourer, was swum, malicious and evil people having raised an ill report of her being a witch.' So much for our dream of village life being innocent and secure!

Chelsworth and Bildeston

*'And how we watched the people, through the seasons, harvest and plough and sow
and plant and reap … and the landscape turn from green to gold to brown …'*
Bob Arbib, *Here We Are Together.*

After so many villages where the houses are gathered around a green, it is a delightful surprise to discover Chelsworth. Here the River Brett has been allowed to dictate the layout, and it encouraged the early builders to line the houses on one side of the river, separated only by fields.

A pair of hump back bridges in red and yellow brick carry the road over the water, and the crossing point is attractive at any time of the year, but especially so at spring when daffodils appear to grow everywhere, right down to the river's edge.

Across the fields stands the church of All Saints, looking rather unhappy that at some time in its history its flintwork has been hidden beneath a layer of cement rendering. In 1746 the churchwardens sold three of the four bells to raise money to repair the steeple.

Today Chelsworth draws visitors who search for peace and beauty. It is hard to believe that during the early 19th century the villagers had to summon the Bow Street Runners to deal with the local hooligans who were a noisy disruptive threat to their tranquillity!

Nearby Bildeston (*inset*) was once a busy wool town. Today there is a wealth of timber and plasterwork for the visitor to admire. Along the High Street are many houses with oversailing upper storeys which date from the 16th century when Bildeston's blue cloth was much in demand. These were the houses where the skilled weavers lived and worked.

Kersey

'One cannot wish that such [harsh] conditions of life should return, but that is no reason for withholding a full mead of admiration for the people that they produced.'
Hugh Farmer, *The Cottage in the Forest*.

Nostalgia for the village way of life is never far from our consciousness: even the most hardened city dwellers know that once their families lived in a community of perhaps no more than 300 people. Those same urban inhabitants also nurse a dream of one day returning to their roots. The village is closer to our national identity than we care to admit. When we consider the village of our dreams Kersey fulfils all the criteria.

The first view of Kersey is never forgotten. Spread before us is the most perfect village imaginable – two lines of timber houses, all different and yet compatible form a palette of washed colours, chosen by an unknown artist to create a masterpiece. The roof line rises and falls with a delicious disregard for symmetry and the tall chimneys puncture the skyline with haphazard and mischievous pleasure. There is usually a wisp of blue smoke too, just enough to remind us that this is no film set, but a settlement where life has been lived and celebrated for over a thousand years. And all around are the rich soils and luxurious greenery of High Suffolk.

The Splash, which is really a tributary of the River Brett, provides a focal point. It flows across the roadway, and passes under a pretty white railed bridge. It is usually teeming with ducks of all sorts and sizes, often with young in well-ordered lines behind them.

Above the village stands the church of St Mary, a gem from the Perpendicular age, complete with fine windows and an impressive porch. The size of the nave reminds us how much larger the village was in the Middle Ages. Kersey's wealth was based on Kersey wool, a hard wearing blue broadcloth, whose reputation was known throughout England.

Polstead and Boxford

'Past half-timbered homes of ancient date, and prosperous-looking rick-surrounded
farmsteads, whose windows gleamed in the golden light.'
James John Hissey, *Tour in a Phaeton Through The Eastern Counties.*

The focal point of this charming and famous village is the great pond, which is appropriate for the name, Polstead, means 'the place of pools'. The houses seem to rise above the water, each row slightly higher than the last, and the timber, brick, thatch and tile form a most pleasing contrast. Across the pool and the River Box there is a brick bridge which links village and church.

The church of St Mary dates from Norman times, and

there are experts who become excited when the talk turns to the brick arches within it, as they could provide evidence that the Normans were using bricks long before they are supposed to have had the skill! At any rate, they are the earliest surviving bricks in England.

Polstead's claim to fame, and the cause of summer coach trips to this day, is a crime which continues to fascinate and disturb – the murder of Maria Marten by William Corder, a farmer's son, in the Red Barn in 1827.

Boxford (*inset*) is still a busy village, if only because the main road passes through it and prevents it opting out of the 20th century. There are many old houses and a great mix of styles and periods. The White Hart Inn was owned by Tornado Smith, a stuntman who built a wall of death in the yard. He rode his motor bike round it, sometimes with his pet lion in the sidecar! When the lion died (of natural causes) it was buried in the front garden – or at least that is the local version of the story.

The church of St Mary contains a touching monument to David Birde, the parson's son, who died in 1606. He is shown asleep in a cot, with his little slippers underneath.

Stoke by Nayland and Pakenham

'We exist only in the landscape, and are creatures of the landscape …'
John Constable, 1836.

Suffolk's wealth of gorgeous villages has unexpectedly resulted in only a few being really well known. Stoke by Nayland on a summer day can stand comparison with any famous Suffolk view, and in its sheer diversity it is probably in a class of its own.

Situated on a hill it surveys the Stour valley, rising above leafy lanes and well established woodland. Those same woods were once the source of much of the timber which now stands shaped and worked as houses, barns and doorways. The Guildhall and The Maltings stand close to the church in School Street, forests of oak in their own right, cleverly constructed to follow the road which falls away sharply down into the valley.

The church of St Mary has a tower 120 feet high, soaring above the landscape, and known to the world as the church which appears on the skyline of many paintings by John Constable. Inside it has all the splendours we have come to expect from a wool church of the Perpendicular period, including a magnificent tower arch and several aristocrats in brass.

Pakenham (*inset*) is not content to have one mill – it must have two – wind and water. In the village is a poignant reminder of the brief visit of the artist Rex Whistler. In 1944 he was stationed nearby, and one rainy day he stood beneath his umbrella and painted an illusion on a long-bricked up bedroom window at the vicarage. To this day we can enjoy the picture of an old parson, with wig and book, glimpsed reading high up in his upstairs study at Mulberry House. Whistler was killed at Normandy soon after.

East Bergholt

*'I associate my "careless boyhood" to all that lies on the banks of the Stour.
They made me a painter, and I am grateful.'* John Constable.

One person is responsible for East Bergholt being a popular tourist attraction, and his name is John Constable. The house where he was born has long since gone, marked only by a plaque on a garden railing, but the studio where in 1802 he first began his career, can still be seen, and it serves as an appropriate reminder of how humble his artistic origins were, for it is very undistinguished!

Some of the inhabitants of East Bergholt did very well out of the wool trade and their fine houses line the main street, often concealed behind beautiful gardens. In the 16th century, during the good times, the influential men of the village decided the time was ripe to take on their rivals in nearby Dedham: they would build a tower to St Mary's which would confirm their rising status.

Unfortunately, it seems likely the money ran out in 1525, and the project had to be abandoned, with the results evident today – a half-built tower. However, they were determined not to lose everything, so the bells intended for the tower were placed in a 'temporary' bell house in the churchyard in 1531. It is still there, and in use today! Some say the bell cage took so long to build because the Devil dismantled the work at night.

Constable took a lifetime to paint a mere nine miles of the River Stour, for the pictures he created along the river, around Flatford Mill, form the core of his achievement and are responsible for his reputation. His family built this mill (*inset*) in 1733, and today it is a centre for field studies.

Tattingstone and Erwarton

'… we in this Suffolk are not so completely given over to prose and turnips as some would have us.' Edward Fitzgerald.

No living village can ever remain the same. Over the centuries enormous changes have taken place in the name of progress, and for the most part they are accepted as necessary, and perhaps even beneficial. Few would wish to return to an age without electricity or running water. But some communities are called upon to accept drastic changes to their entire way of life. Tattingstone was a quiet village to the south of Ipswich, whose peace was only disturbed by the arrival and departure of the daily coach which paused at the old inn. Today there is no road and no inn, but instead there is a vast expanse of water, for this is now the site of Alton Reservoir, which has flooded the valley and destroyed the past.

One of the casualties of the great flood was Tattingstone Hall – ironically it had always been moated! Edward White lived there and in 1790 he built what is known as the Tattingstone Wonder. From one side it is a small country church, complete with tower, but from the other it is a group of farm workers' cottages. White is supposed to have said that as his neighbours gawped at nothing, they might as well gawp at something!

Erwarton Hall (*inset*) stands near Shotley, which was once a great naval training establishment. The Hall was the official residence of the Royal Navy Commanding Officer for most of this century.

The present building dates from 1575, but the unusual gatehouse is earlier, and is quite the most interesting feature to survive from the Hall's famous connection.

Local legend says Anne Boleyn stayed at the Hall as a child, and later entertained Henry VIII there. After her execution her body was brought to Erwarton church. Her heart was placed in a casket, which was found during renovations in 1837.

48

Pin Mill and Chelmondiston

'… to speak cautiously [this] is one of the most beautiful salt rivers in the world.'
John Kirby, 1735.

Every pub has to have a licence, but few can make such a fine claim as the famous Butt and Oyster Inn at Pin Mill – it had one of the first ever issued, in 1553. No doubt the price of a drink has gone up a lot since then, but the drinking capacity of the local river men has probably remained the same.

This is the point on the River Orwell where sea-going ships used to off-load their cargo onto barges for the remainder of the journey to Ipswich. For centuries this has been a place of intense activity, and not all of it has been legal, for Pin Mill is closely associated with the world of smugglers and Revenue Officers.

The River Orwell is still one of England's most beautiful rivers and many of the visitors throughout the summer have no intentions of getting their feet wet ! Pin Mill is a popular tourist attraction, particularly in early July when the barge races take place.

Arthur Ransome, the children's author, loved Pin Mill, and lived in nearby Alma Cottage. He kept his boat, the *Nancy Blackett* here, and his book *We Didn't Mean To Go To Sea* was about a voyage down the Orwell and into the Great North Sea.

Much of the coastline here is lined with oak and alder trees, the property of the National Trust. It is a wonderful place to sit and reflect on the passage of time, disturbed only by the clink of beer glasses and the rattle of rigging wires on the barge masts. Difficult to believe that here was the last recorded outbreak of bubonic plague!

Chelmondiston seems to stretch for miles along the road, but there are many lovely houses with enormous gardens (*inset*). The church in the village was destroyed by a Flying Bomb during the Second World War which seems a bit of bad luck as there are so many miles of field and water for it to have hit.

Tuddenham St Martin and Sproughton

'On a clear day – and they are mostly clear days in this part of the world – you can see as far as you can bear to see, and sometimes farther.' Ronald Blythe, *Akenfield.*

Tuddenham St Martin is to the north of Ipswich, and occupies a valley formed by the River Fynn. The road descends a steep hill beside the church and slips past a row of absolutely delightful cottages. There is a profusion of flowers in season, and every one proclaims the care and affection with which they are regarded by their owners. Once they were intended for agricultural labourers, and probably were functional rather than decorative. Now they are much sought after, as being within a few minutes of the centre of Ipswich, but wholly apart from the urban sprawl which is still a mile or two distant.

The view of the village from the north is dominated by the church of St Martin, and can surely have changed little since it was built in the 15th century. Nearby stands the busy Fountain Inn which remains as popular today as it was when the church builders dropped in for a drink!

Another village which has found a way of coping with the proximity of Ipswich is Sproughton (pronounced *Sprawton*) and in some ways it has had an even more demanding challenge, for it stands amidst the western industrial estates, and large factories and warehouses are within its view. However, it is possible to walk beside the River Gipping and find a line of contemplative fisherfolk, oblivious to the wider world, and clearly enjoying the peace and quiet of this idyllic spot. From their river bank 'pitch' they sit opposite the Georgian mill (*inset*) which employed the barges which plied the river from Ipswich to Stowmarket, once it was made navigable in 1793. The mill stopped working in 1947, an event not unrelated to the last barge gliding past in 1930.

Grundisburgh and Boulge

'The last footfall dies into silence. The stillness tingles with the aftermath of noise.'
Adrian Bell, *Corduroy.*

The River Lark flows across the village green of Grundisburgh, and creates an attractive picture of old and new in harmony. The church of St Mary is considered to have a superb hammer beam roof, which says something for the wealth and status of this community many centuries ago. There was once a flint tower but that collapsed during the 16th century, and when in the course of time a benefactor called Robert Thring left money to make good the loss it was rebuilt in red brick.

The countryside beyond Grundisburgh is exceptionally pretty, with a surprising number of small fields and scores of woods and valleys. Many of the cottages are still coloured in the traditional pink wash, which is supposed to include blood in the mix!

The village of Boulge would not be known as widely as it is, had it not been for the famous occupant of Boulge Hall. Edward Fitzgerald's family came to Boulge from Wherstead. They had problems getting on with one another and young Edward moved from Boulge Hall into an attractive cottage which stands just outside the park gates. There he lived the life of a Victorian gentleman, free of the need to work, and able to enjoy good food, wine and agreeable company. He was the centre of a group of local cultured characters who enjoyed being described as the Woodbridge Wits.

He is honoured to this day for his translation in verse of the *Rubaiyat of Omar Khayyam*, a 2,500 year old poem about love, wine and death. His grave in Boulge churchyard (*inset*) stands beside the family mausoleum. Planted at the head are six roses from Naishapur in Persia, taken from Khayyam's tomb.

Great Bealings and Coddenham

'Many of the villages may be fairly said to nestle into the country scene.'
Alan Jobson, *Suffolk Villages.*

St Mary's church, Great Bealings (*opposite*), stands perfectly amid the folds of rich arable land in this picturesque part of Suffolk. A line of noble trees stretches from the churchyard down to the hump back bridge which carries the country lane over a tributary of the River Fynn. It is a lovely scene and as the seasons change it loses none of its power to impress and move. In spring the daffodils appear to create a carpet of perpetual movement, and at times the flag of St George, fluttering above the church tower, can be glimpsed through the trees, accompanied by the sonorous tones of the deep voiced bells.

In the beginning there were two communities here, Belinges Magna and Belinges Parva, and it was only in 1674 that the modern names became current. The two villages of Bealings are separated by a mile of pretty roadway and each continues to assert its independence.

Thomas Seckford of Woodbridge, who rose to wealth and power at the court of Queen Elizabeth, lived at Seckford Hall close by, and he did not forget these villages, for he built the porch at St Mary's and raised a grand memorial to his parents in All Saints, Little Bealings. His family home is now a splendid country hotel, complete with the obligatory golf course.

Coddenham's main street is worth a good look, but unfortunately it is a dangerous thing to do as the traffic roars past and has little time for gracious cottages (*inset*) and flowering gardens. There is a richness of styles in a short space, most of them delightfully haphazard and formed around rich timber beams. There were once many more pubs in this village, and one of them, the Crown Inn, was the home of one Wodehouse, an archer knighted by Henry V on the field of Agincourt. Such is the span of time in rural Suffolk!

Debenham

'[In Debenham] with abundant cheap labour the standard of farming was remarkably high. The horses, the famous Suffolk punches, were excellent.'
James Cornish, *Reminiscences of Country Life.*

Nothing is ever straightforward. Even if it is agreed that the River Deben rises just beyond Debenham, it is still open to debate what the word means. Some say it is just the 'deep one', while others point to even earlier Celtic roots. Today the river begins its 15 mile journey to the North Sea amid these small hills, and sweeps past the houses and gardens, even running along the road after a heavy storm.

There is a curious age difference apparent along the street, and while on one side there are ancient timber shops, many with alleyways beside them for the carts which once supplied them, on the other side – where stands St Mary's church – the houses are of brick, and clearly of another, later period. In a word, Fire! There was a village conflagration here in 1744 and it destroyed 38 houses around the church, but fortunately it did not cross the road and so old and newer have confronted each other ever since.

Evidence of the age of this place is provided by the church which still shows Saxon stonework at the base of the tower. The alternate long and short blocks have been mute witnesses to a thousand years of faith and loyalty.

The greens are Debenham's good fortune for they open up the street plan, and ensure the buildings have space to be appreciated. The old Guildhall is one of the very best of these, and once it was the centre of life in Debenham. It is now a gallery, and overlooks others which sell books and antiques.

Earl Soham and Brandeston

'The English landscape at its subtlest and loveliest is to be seen in the County of Suffolk.' John T. Appleby, *Suffolk Summer.*

As befits a village which seems to extend for miles, Earl Soham encompasses many periods of building, and manages to include no less than three separate village greens. It is built along a number of sharp bends, each offering a series of views which are a delight to behold.

The word Soham indicates a marsh, and the Earl is a reminder of the Bigod family, Earls of Norfolk and builders of Framlingham Castle. On the main village green, at a bend in the road, stands a contemporary wooden village sign, depicting a falconer, an echo of the aristocratic sporting association which continues into our present times.

On the outskirts stands the 13th century church of St Mary with its 15th century tower. The group of buildings around the churchyard emphasises the importance of the developments undertaken in the Georgian period, when the residents of Earl Soham must have been reasonably affluent, and very ambitious.

Brandeston is another of the villages which stands besides the River Deben. In the 16th century Andrew Revett built a country house overlooking the river, and it survives to this day, now as a Preparatory School for Framlingham College. There are many lovely cottages strung out along the village street (*inset*).

The village sign includes a picture of a body on a gallows, which takes us back to the frightening times of the 17th century and the Witchfinder General, Matthew Hopkins. The rector of All Saints, John Lowes, was accused of witchcraft, tortured, survived ordeal by drowning, and so was hanged at Bury St Edmunds. He was 80 years old.

Kettleburgh and Easton

'It is evening, and the swallows are flying low by the river. I am sitting by the water's edge, under the bank, and the swallows come skimming over it and flash past my head …' Adrian Bell, *Men and the Fields*.

The landscape we enjoy today was formed millions of years ago, of course, but the villages which are dotted over it owe their existence to the rivers, and the River Deben winds its way to the sea, giving life to the dozen or so settlements it created and sustains. In the olden days there was a water mill at Kettleburgh.

Probably because the ground beside it was marshy for much of the year, the Deben has not encouraged the building of a roadway which runs with it to the sea, a great boon, for the land remains largely unspoilt. There are a number of crossing points, some of them no more than narrow hump backed bridges constructed in times when traffic was slower and less demanding. Kettleburgh has just such a bridge and it stands amid beautiful water meadows, reflected in the water, along with willows, lilies, and well-fed cattle.

The next village is Easton, which is famous for two things: a two-mile crinkle-crankle wall, and Easton Farm Park. It was in 1870 that the Duke of Hamilton created his farm which was to embody the very latest good practice in farm management. There was no need for a farm house as the Duke lived in the nearby Hall. Today the farm is still open to the public, and in particular it attracts large numbers of children who learn how a real farm works.

Saxtead Green

*'Suffolk, the birthplace and inspiration of Constable and Gainsborough, the loveliest of
English painters; the home of Crabbe, the most English of poets.'*
Benjamin Britten, Speech 1951.

Just occasionally the countryside can provide us with a view which is so unspoilt and satisfying that for a moment the entire world becomes a better place. Saxtead Green (*opposite*) is one such place. The scent of new mown hay is never to be forgotten, and here it rises from one of Suffolk's prettiest greens, surrounded by cottages

and bungalows. Throughout the summer days an ice cream van obligingly offers its wares to the carloads of children unable to resist the call. But the focal point for everyone is Saxtead Mill, a dazzlingly white weatherboarded post mill, with a distinct blue fantail, that rears above the hedgerows and dominates the view for several miles.

The first mill on this site has been traced back to 1287, but the present one dates from 1796. It represents the supreme development of the mill and is bewilderingly complex to the layman. A terrifyingly steep ladder provides access to the interior, which on a windy day is sufficient to cause alarm. Once inside not an inch is wasted, as wheels, cogs and axles take up all the space not used by grain bins and ladder ways. The mill ceased to work in 1947 when it was acquired by the forerunner of English Heritage.

As a reminder of less happy times the church of All Saints contains within its porch stocks and a whipping post. On the village green is the Old Mill House, a fine pub which has moved with the times and in addition to the usual freehouse fare serves excellent meals and provides a garden for family use.

Snape

*'I found that the delicate music of the Suffolk coast … still had more charm for me
than the great brass bands of natural scenery, the Alps or the Dolomites.'*
Sir Kenneth Clark, *Tribute to Britten on his 50th birthday.*

Even for a county with such an exceptional coastline as Suffolk, the views at Snape are impossible to describe or anticipate. There is a moment in the day when the visitor can stand on the bank of the River Alde, with the Maltings Concert Hall at his back, and look over the great expanse of still water towards the church of Iken and truly wonder if this is not paradise. The only sounds in the world are of the wind parting the reeds and the wildfowl screaming their indignant warnings. A thousand years is wiped away in that instant. No wonder this place has inspired some of the greatest artists and musicians of our time.

The sea may be only five miles distant as the crow flies, but for those in boats it is three times as far, for the Alde (*inset*) has first to unite with the Ore, and so pursue its journey to the North Sea.

It was in 1854 that the Maltings were built and for a century they served the farms which brought in barley for malting. Graceful barges from London came up the river and moored off the quayside, awaiting another cargo, and so the trade went on. In 1967 the Maltings took on a new lease of life after years of neglect, when they became the world famous Snape Maltings Concert Hall, established and inspired by the composer Benjamin Britten and the tenor Peter Pears. A fire destroyed the hall but within a year it was rebuilt and continues to this day as one of the finest concert halls for recording in Europe.

Benjamin Britten composed his opera *Peter Grimes* while living in the Old Mill at Snape, and his music evokes the sounds of the marshlands and the lives of the people who lived by fishing.

Orford

'On a still day, the light can have the delicate outline of a Japanese picture.'
Imogen Holst, *Britten.*

There was a time when Orford was a town of some size and importance, with a port which brought it a large and steady revenue. All that changed as the coastline altered shape, and a great shingle spit grew across its harbour mouth. The Ness is now six miles long and in the care of the National Trust.

Today Orford is a busy tourist centre, dominated by a superb and unusual castle (*inset*) and blessed with lines of grand houses and quaint cottages, all focused on a

quayside and river bank which seem almost too good to be true.

The castle is a work of great complexity, and when it was constructed in the middle of the 12th century by Henry II there must have been many who shook their heads at the new design. It was intended to inhibit the treasonable activities of the powerful Bigod family, who lorded it over East Anglia from nearby Framlingham. The walls are so thick there are rooms cut into them.

One early visitor was the legendary Orford Merman, half man, half fish, who was caught out at sea and brought back. His treatment was so cruel that at the first opportunity he fled back to sea.

The church of St Bartholomew is important to lovers of contemporary music for it saw the first performances of several of Benjamin Britten's works, including *Noyes Fludde* (1958) and *Curlew River* (1964), as part of the world famous Aldeburgh Festival.

Lovers of good food inevitably are drawn to the Butley Oysterage, which has founded its reputation on the very finest oysters and smoked salmon. Equally important is the Jolly Sailor Inn in Quay Street which still offers simple entertainment of a traditional variety.

Kelsale and Rendham

'For it is the mind which creates the world about us … my eyes will never see what is beheld by yours.' George Gissing, *The Private Papers of Henry Ryecroft*.

Even a small village is entitled to suburbs, it appears, and throughout Suffolk there are hamlets and isolated offshoots which wear their names with pride, and resent being lumped together. Kelsale is situated to the north of Saxmundham, and around it are places with names such as Dorley's Corner, Carlton and Curlew Green. Is there a more beautiful and evocative name for a settlement than this last which nestles at the end of a lane between two main roads, unseen and unsuspected by the impatient drivers who speed past?

The church of St Mary and St Peter looks down on the houses from its hill, and is approached through a most unusual and amusing lych gate, which resembles an upturned boat. In the village is the Old Guildhall of 1495 which is now used as a Teachers' Centre. Here as elsewhere, the knack of finding new uses for old buildings has proved to be a village speciality.

Rendham (*inset*) has earned its moment in history on two occasions, and so can consider itself fortunate. The poet George Crabbe was Rector here and during his incumbency wrote some of his most famous poem, *The Borough*, which includes the story of Peter Grimes. In 1907 a boy swimming in the River Alde at Rendham Bridge discovered a Roman head of the Emperor Claudius in the water. It is thought to have been smashed and thrown away during Boudicca's revolt in AD 61. Now that is a village time span!

Dunwich and Theberton

'This town is a testimony to the decay of public things.'
Daniel Defoe, *Tour through Britain.*

It is almost impossible to stand on the shore at Dunwich without being moved to reflect on really serious things. It has that effect on visitors. For this was once a great city, a centre of life for generations of East Anglians.

At the time of the Norman Conquest in 1066 Dunwich had a population of over 3,000 which made it three times the size of Ipswich. Within its extensive walls were 18 churches, and in the harbour was a merchant fleet of 80 vessels.

In 1328 a great storm swallowed up 400 houses and three churches in a single night. The harbour became blocked, the trade moved away, and still the sea took its tribute. Over the centuries the city simply died as the waves cut away the wharfs, houses, gardens, and roads. Even today there are those who look out across the waves and imagine silent, subterranean streets, lofty towers and eerily persistent church bells. But the truth is simpler, the people had gone before the final tide arrived, and they had carried away their valuables to higher ground and temporary safety.

A great monastery stood on the landward side of the city. Fragments of Grey Friars remain, poised on the edge of the city cliffs, awaiting their call to crash into the sea.

In the little village of Theberton (*inset*) the church, with its thatched roof and round tower, is full of memories of the Doughty family, who lived in the Hall. Charles Montague Doughty explored Arabia in the 19th century and his classic account *Travels in Arabia Deserta* has been described by his admirers as the best travel book ever written.

In the churchyard is a curious monument. A Zeppelin was shot down over Theberton in 1917 and the crew were buried in a row of graves which were tended with respect by the villagers for many years.

Yoxford and Middleton

'I love the wide sky, the wonderful sunsets, and the loneliness of the estuaries. I love the marshes, the birds, the reeds, and the smell of the sea everywhere.' P. D. James.

On the outskirts of Yoxford, set back from the busy A12 trunk road, stands a large house, now a restaurant, which bears the name Satis House. Local tradition is keen to perpetuate the story that when Charles Dickens travelled this road as a coach passenger on one of his journalistic assignments he would have noted the name, and allowed it to resurface much later as the scene of Miss Haversham's eccentricity in *Great Expectations*. The house and the name existed long before the novel.

In the centre of Yoxford, against the churchyard stands a lovely wrought iron signpost, whose hands indicate the directions of London, Framlingham and Yarmouth. As it dates from the 1830s it is not too fanciful to suppose that Dickens would have seen it as his stagecoach sped past.

Along the main street, near the Post Office is a pink house with a number of Georgian features – all painted on the brickwork! Not only has the artist included a pot of flowers at the window but a peacock struts around the corner, permanently on guard. Another house has a metal balcony which in spring and summer is a blaze of colour from a cluster of flower pots and hanging baskets.

Rivalry between villages is nothing new, and even the smallest things could provoke feuds and discontent. In Middleton churchyard there were once two churches, for strictly speaking this is the parish of Middleton cum Fordley. Apparently the bells of Fordley summoning their faithful to worship so upset the pious folk of Middleton that they managed to get the rival church pulled down in the mid 17th century.

Like so many villages, in Middleton (*inset*) the last of the shops has given up the unequal fight with the supermarkets, and become a private house. But at least the school goes on, and the roll call shows no signs of declining, if only because several neighbouring villages contribute to the numbers. The Middleton Bell is well known for fine ale, good food and enjoyable singing so the staples of rural life appear secure.

Wenhaston and Walpole

'The East Anglian is, of course, a solid man. Lots of beef and beer, tempered with east wind have gone into the making of him.'
J. B. Priestley, *English Journey.*

St Peter's, Wenhaston is famous for its Doom (*opposite*) – a medieval wall painting, dating from about 1480, which shows the Last Judgement and the division of souls between Heaven and Hell, God and the Devil. Most churches had brightly decorated walls, and like stained glass, they were used to teach illiterate congregations their Bible stories. Wenhaston's was hastily covered with whitewash in 1549 when the government attacked such 'wicked' images. In 1889 the Doom was rediscovered when rain water washed off the whitewash, exposing a unique piece of East Anglian art!

Walpole chapel (*inset*) began as a house in 1607, but was converted to a chapel as early as 1649. While the builders were at work, Charles I was tried and executed. The chapel was enlarged in 1698, and a ship's mast was placed in the centre to support the roof. The lovely windows, candelabra, pulpit and lectern date from this time. Lines of numbered box pews soon followed and were for the better-off members of the congregation. Folk of simpler means occupied the gallery which extends around three sides of the hall.

When Samuel Habergham preached to the first congregation of Independents in 1649 he could not doubt that Suffolk would remain loyal to the Puritan beliefs, but by 1662 his successor Samuel Manning had no such confidence. The Act of Uniformity branded the people who gathered to worship in this beautiful building dangerous and treasonable. For doing so they were fined, imprisoned or transported. Their faith enabled them to endure, and even today the silence of this chapel can inspire and humble the visitor. It was closed in 1970 but there are still annual services, and the last incumbent is a wonderful guide!

Somerleyton and Blundeston

'There is nothing half so green that I know anywhere, as the grass of that churchyard;
nothing half so shady as its trees; nothing half so quiet as its tombstones.'
Charles Dickens, *David Copperfield*.

The Victorians were nothing if not adventurous and ambitious. Sir Morton Peto may stand as the epitome of his kind. He made his fortune building railways at a time when the country simply could not get enough of them. So extensive was his fortune that by 1851 he was able to underwrite the Great Exhibition.

Somerleyton Hall was built to proclaim Peto's importance. He even took over the bell tower originally

intended for the Houses of Parliament, but rejected in favour of Big Ben.

On the wide green Peto created a village of mock Tudor cottages, many crowned with thatch and quaint brick chimneys. As a vision of the English idyll it fulfils many of the criteria, but the obvious uniformity of date is hard to overlook. Perhaps aware of this, the church was rebuilt in the conventional style.

Further along the road is Blundeston – or Blunderstone, as Dickens calls it. Here the world believes David Copperfield was born, and from here he set out for Yarmouth in a cart dreamily controlled by Barkis (who was willing). The village sign depicts Davy on the eve of his journey to London. St Mary's church, with its Norman archway (*inset*), appears in the novel, although the sundial over the door is of a later period. It is impossible to mention the existence of a maximum security prison nearby without appearing to have very poor taste, but in mitigation there are those who claim its site, Blundeston Lodge, was the inspiration for Thomas Gray's *Elegy in a Country Churchyard*.